Food and Festivals

ITALY

Saviour Pirotta

RAINTREE
STECK-VAUGHN
PUBLISHERS
A Steck Vaughn Company

Austin, Texas

Food and Festivals

ITALY

Other titles:

The Caribbean • China • India
Mexico • West Africa

Cover photograph: An Italian food shop

Title page: A float at the Viareggio carnival

Contents page: A young stilt walker at the Venice carnival

Published by Raintree Steck-Vaughn Publishers,
an imprint of Steck-Vaughn Company

Printed in Italy. Bound in the United States.
1 2 3 4 5 6 7 8 9 0 03 02 01 00 99

Library of Congress Cataloging-in-Publication Data
Pirotta, Saviour.
Italy / Saviour Pirotta.
    p.   cm.—(Food and festivals)
Includes bibliographical references and index.
Summary: Discusses some of the foods enjoyed in Italy and describes special foods that are part of such specific celebrations as All Saints' Day, the Festival of Saint Dominic, and Carnival.
ISBN 0-8172-5760-8 (hard)
ISBN 0-7398-0958-X (soft)
1. Cookery, Italian—Juvenile literature.
2. Food habits—Italy—Juvenile literature.
3. Italy—Social life and customs—Juvenile literature.
4. Festivals—Italy—Juvenile literature.
[1. Cookery, Italian. 2. Food habits—Italy. 3. Festivals—Italy. 4. Holidays—Italy. 5. Italy—Social life and customs.]
I. Title. II. Series.
TX723.P55   1999
641.5945—dc21   98-46691

CONTENTS

Italy and Its Food

SWITZERLAND

AUSTRIA

FRANCE

AOSTA VALLEY

PIEDMONT

LOMBARDY

SLOVENIA

Italy's place in the world

ITALY

CROATIA

BOSNIA-HERZEGOVINA

Verona

PO VALLEY

Venice

ITALY

LIGURIA

Viareggio

Florence

A D R I A T I C   S E A

Perugia

N

Lake Bolsena

ABRUZZO

Rome

MOLISE

PUGLIA

CAMPANIA

Putignano

Naples

Taranto

SARDINIA

0 — 200 km

0 — 125 miles

Cagliari

M E D I T E R R A N E A N   S E A

CALABRIA

SICILY

I O N I A N   S E A

WHEAT

Wheat and corn are the most important cereals grown in Italy. Different kinds of wheat are used for making pasta, bread, and cakes.

FRUIT

Apples, peaches, and citrus fruits are important crops. Every region in Italy has its own vineyards, where grapes are grown for wine.

CHEESE AND MILK

Grated Parmesan cheese is sprinkled on spaghetti, and mozzarella cheese, made from buffalo milk, is used as a topping for pizzas. Milk is also used to make ice cream.

VEGETABLES

Italy produces many different vegetables. Tomatoes are made into various sauces. Onions, peppers, and garlic give food a lot of flavor.

OLIVES

Olive trees grow in most parts of Italy. The olives are pressed to make olive oil, one of the most popular ingredients in Italian cooking.

MEAT

Italians eat a lot of fresh meat, such as chicken, beef, veal, lamb, and pork. They also enjoy the meat of wild animals, such as rabbits and birds.

Food and Farming

Italy is a long, narrow country in southern Europe. In the northern part of the country there is plenty of rain, and cereals such as wheat and corn grow well. In the south, the weather is much hotter. Lemons, grapes, and olives can be grown.

Delicious Italian foods, such as pizza, pasta, and ice cream, are a part of everyday life around the world. Many people forget that these foods come from Italy.

▼ A farmer checks the harvest in an Italian wheat field.

▲ Traditional Italian bread is baked in wood-burning ovens. Many bakeries are run by families.

Cereals and rice

Wheat and corn are the most important cereal grains grown in Italy. Wheat is used for making bread, cakes, pizza, and pasta. Italians buy pasta fresh or dried. Some even make their own at home.

Rice is grown in some regions. The most famous rice comes from the Po Valley. It is cooked with cheese and garlic to make a creamy dish called *risotto*.

Cheese and milk

The mountains and fertile plains of northern Italy are good for grazing cows. Many kinds of cheese are made from their milk. The Aosta Valley is known for cheeses such as *robiola* and *fontina*. Nearby in Lombardy, dairy farmers make *mascarpone*, *gorgonzola*, and *taleggio*.

Farther south, in the region of Abruzzo, farmers raise sheep to make special cheeses such as *pecorino*.

▲ Farmers in the town of Eboli, near Naples, make *mozzarella* cheese from buffalo milk.

▼ Buffaloes in Agropoli, near Naples. Buffalo milk is not drunk but used only to make cheese.

FRUIT AND VEGETABLES

The Italians hold many festivals to celebrate the different fruits and vegetables grown in their country. In the region of Liguria, there are eggplant, lemon, cherry, strawberry, and chestnut festivals.

Another chestnut festival is held on the island of Sardinia. The people of Aritzo, a town surrounded by chestnut groves, welcome visitors with boiled and roasted chestnut treats.

Fruit and vegetables

Italy produces grapes, olives, and citrus fruits, such as oranges and lemons. Olives grow in most parts of the country. They can be eaten or pressed to make olive oil.

Italian farmers produce a large variety of crops, depending on the climate. In the southern region of Campania, where the soil is rich and there are long, hot summers, farmers grow plum tomatoes. In other regions asparagus, beans, cauliflower, onions, and garlic are grown.

▲ Farmers from Venice show off their harvest in a gondola, a type of boat.

9

▲ Women in southern Italy prepare cured meats to be used in cooked dishes, salads, and sandwiches.

Meat

Italians enjoy a wide range of meat in their dishes. In the north, farmers raise cows, so people cook a lot of beef and veal. Pigs are also raised. Pork is eaten all over the country, either fresh or cured as sausages and ham. Farther south, where the land is drier, farmers raise sheep, poultry, rabbits, and goats.

Fish

Most of Italy is surrounded by the Mediterranean and Adriatic seas. People in coastal towns eat fresh fish and seafood. In the north, people catch fish from lakes, rivers, and streams. Anchovies, swordfish, tuna, squid, octopus, and small herring are popular ingredients in Italian cooking.

▼ A fishing boat prepares to leave the harbor of Trapani on the island of Sicily.

FESTIVAL AT SEA

There are many local fish festivals in Italy. The parade at the festival of San Cataldo in Taranto actually takes place at sea. People at the festival eat fried fish as part of the celebrations.

Family Celebrations

Most Italians are Roman Catholics. Catholicism is a Christian religion, headed by the Pope. Mary, the mother of Jesus, is particularly important to Catholics.

Catholics celebrate the most important events of their lives with special religious ceremonies. Baptisms, weddings, and funerals all take place in church. Happy occasions are always followed by a huge party, to which friends and family are invited.

Italians have *feste*, ▶ which are special days to honor saints. These girls are celebrating the festival of Saint Efisio, in Cagliari, Sardinia.

▼ A procession in Puglia to honor Saint Cosmas and Saint Damian

ALL SAINTS' DAY

All Saints' Day takes place on November 1. Catholics honor dead people who have led a good life. Children eat special cookies shaped like lima beans. They are called *fave dolce romane* (sweet Roman beans, or bean-shaped cookies). There is a recipe for the cookies on page 17.

Weddings

Italian weddings are very lavish. The long ceremony in church is followed by a meal that can have up to fourteen courses. Meals vary from region to region but usually start with an elegant *antipasto*, such as Parma ham. This course may be followed by soup, a small pasta dish, chicken, rabbit, or fish.

Sugared almonds, called *confetti*, are found at every wedding. Sometimes they are arranged so that they look like bunches of flowers and are put next to the place cards on the table.

◀ Many Italians have their wedding feasts outside. These people are celebrating in their hometown of Calabria.

At some weddings, the *confetti* are wrapped in little bags and handed out by the bridesmaids. Each parcel is called a *bomboniera*. There are five almonds in each *bomboniera*. They stand for health, happiness, wealth, children, and a long life.

▲ The wedding cake is usually a light sponge cake, flavored with a liqueur and a special filling called *zuppa inglese*. The cake is covered with whipped cream.

▲ Cookies shaped like dried beans for All Saints' Day

Local festivals

The Italian calendar is packed with local festivals. Most of them, like the Festival of Saint Dominic in Cocullo, Abruzzo, are held in honor of patron saints. There are processions and fireworks. Snacks and delicious Italian ice cream are sold from street stands.

Many festivals celebrate crops and harvests. In the town of Collelongo, Abruzzo, there is a cooking pot festival. The pots are blessed by a local priest and a prize is given to the owner of the best saucepan.

SAINT DOMINIC

Many Italians believe that Saint Dominic protects them from snakebite. During the Festival of Saint Dominic, a statue covered with snakes is paraded around the streets. Five girls follow the statue. They carry special sweet pastry rings in baskets on their heads. After the festival, the pastry rings are given to the men who took part in the parade.

Everyone from the fishing town ▶ of Marta, on Lake Bolsena, comes to the yearly fish festival. There is a procession of fishermen, and children push wheelbarrows of fruit and vegetables.

Bean-shaped Cookies

INGREDIENTS (makes 12)

2/3 cup (100 g) all-purpose flour

6 Tablespoons (90 g) butter, softened

1/4 cup (50 g) granulated sugar

1 egg

2 oz. (50 g) ground almonds

1/2 teaspoon powdered cinnamon

Zest of half a lemon, grated

1 Tablespoon confectioner's sugar

EQUIPMENT

Mixing bowl
Wooden spoon
Whisk
Small mixing bowl
Egg beater

Grater
Chopping board
Knife
Baking sheet
Spatula

Put the flour and butter in the mixing bowl and mix with the wooden spoon until smooth. Whisk the egg in the small bowl.

Add the sugar, almonds, cinnamon, beaten egg, and lemon zest to the flour. Mix to make a smooth dough. Add a little more flour if it is sticky.

Roll the dough into a 6-in. (15-cm) long sausage, and cut into 12 slices. With clean hands, pinch each slice into a lima bean shape and flatten slightly.

Put the cookies on a greased baking tray. Bake for 15 minutes at 350° F (180° C) or until golden brown. When cool, sprinkle with confectioner's sugar.

Always be careful with hot ovens. Ask an adult to help you.

Christmas and New Year's

Christmas is the most important festival in Italy. It celebrates the day when Jesus was born. Each house is decorated with a *presepio*, which is a nativity scene filled with little statues. Nativity scenes are also set up in churches and near famous landmarks. In some towns, people dress up as characters from the Christmas story.

▲ A Roman Catholic priest celebrates Christmas Eve Mass in the famous church of Aracoeli in Rome.

◄ The main figures in a *presepio* are Jesus, Mary, and Joseph. There are shepherds and animals around them.

▲ *Panettone,* a traditional Italian cake with dried fruit

Christmas food

Many Italians fast for twenty-four hours before having a traditional dinner on Christmas Eve. Meals vary from region to region. Some people have fish and seafood stew served with vegetables. Others enjoy lamb, turkey, or spaghetti with anchovies.

Two more big meals are eaten on Christmas Day and New Year's Eve. The New Year's Eve menu might include raisin bread, turkey, rabbit, and pasta. People in certain regions eat a special lentil and sausage dish.

New Year's and Epiphany

The Christmas celebrations end on January 6, the Epiphany. On this day, people remember the three wise men who visited baby Jesus.

Children wait for the Befana, an old woman who brings presents for good children (a bit like Santa Claus). Naughty children are supposed to be given a lump of coal. But the Befana knows that all children are sometimes good and sometimes naughty. She leaves everyone a lump of coal as well as some treats.

NEW YEAR'S EVE

On New Year's Eve, Italians throw old furniture and junk out of the window. This is believed to get rid of bad luck and make way for better times.

▼ Lentils are supposed to bring you more money in the New Year. See the recipe opposite to make this lucky lentil and sausage dish.

Lentils and Sausage

INGREDIENTS (for 4)

$^1/_2$ lb. (250 g) red lentils
1 Tablespoon olive oil
1 small onion, finely chopped
1 stalk celery, chopped
$^1/_2$ medium-sized carrot, sliced
2 Tablespoons tomato paste
1 cup chicken stock
A pinch of dried sage
$^1/_2$ lb. (250 g) salami or pepperoni

EQUIPMENT

Sieve
Saucepan
Chopping board
Knife
Frying pan with lid
Wooden spoon
Ladle

Wash the lentils, using a sieve. Cook them in boiling water until soft but firm. Chop the onion, celery, and carrot.

Fry the chopped onion in the oil until soft. Add the chopped celery and carrot. Cook on a low heat with the lid on for 10 minutes.

Drain the lentils and add them to the vegetables in the pan. Stir in the tomato paste, the stock, and the sage.

Cook for 3 more minutes, then serve mixed with the salami, sliced into small pieces $^1/_4$ in. (1 cm) thick.

Always be careful with hot liquids and pans. Ask an adult to help you.

21

Carnival

▼ A young stilt walker at the Venice carnival

Carnival is an ancient festival. Before Italy became a Christian country, carnival was a festival to celebrate the fertility of the land. Today most Catholics see it as a last chance to have fun and enjoy rich foods before the fasting period of Lent. People go to costume parties and balls, dance in the streets, and share delicious food.

These girls ▶ at the Venice carnival are enjoying ice cream, a popular festival food.

Carnival in Italy has its own special food. Fried strips of pastry called *chiacchiere* are very popular in Piedmont. They are eaten dusted with confectioner's sugar. In Sicily, children eat *cannoli*, sweet pastry tubes filled with sweetened cheese. People in Florence prefer *schiacciata di carnevale,* a delicious cake decorated with a chocolate lily.

▼ Some artists in Viareggio spend the whole year making floats for the carnival.

THE VIAREGGIO CARNIVAL

The carnival in the city of Viareggio has a special parade with papier-mâché statues on floats. The statues all look like famous Italian people, but they are made to look ugly. Children ride on the floats and throw confetti and candy into the crowd.

FARINELLA

Many people at the Putignano carnival dress up as a character called Farinella. His costume is made of brightly colored rags and his hat jingles with little bells. Farinella is named after a stew that poor farmers used to make a long time ago. It had chickpeas and barley in it.

▼ Read the recipe opposite to see how to make minestrone soup, a popular Lenten dish.

Lent

The last day of carnival is called Fat Tuesday. The next day is Ash Wednesday, the beginning of Lent.

Lent lasts for forty days before Easter. Christians spend time thinking about how they can become better people. Many give up luxury foods to remember how Jesus fasted for forty days in the desert. On Fridays, they often eat meat-free meals such as minestrone soup or pasta. Some children give up desserts and candy.

Minestrone Soup

EQUIPMENT

Chopping board
Knife
$1^1/_2$ qt. saucepan
Wooden spoon

Large Pyrex measuring cup
Ladle

INGREDIENTS (serves 4)

- 1 Tablespoon olive oil
- 1 small onion, finely chopped
- 1 medium-sized potato, diced
- 1 stalk celery, chopped
- 2 heaping tablespoons of carrots or frozen peas
- 2 Tablespoons French-cut beans
- 2 oz. (55 g) pasta shapes or broken spaghetti
- 1 Tablespoon chopped fresh parsley or dried parsley
- 2 Tablespoons Grated Parmesan cheese

Heat the olive oil in a saucepan and cook the onions until they start to turn brown. Add the potato and celery. Cook for 6 or 7 minutes.

Slowly and carefully add two cups of water, using the measuring cup, bring to a boil and simmer for 15 minutes.

Put in the rest of the vegetables and the pasta. Simmer for about 10 minutes, until the mixture is soft, but not mushy.

Stir in the parsley and the Parmesan, and serve.

Be careful when you are frying and serving hot liquids. Ask an adult to help.

Easter

On Good Friday, Catholics remember the day Jesus died on the cross. There are processions with people dressed as characters from the four Gospels. Men in robes carry heavy statues showing scenes from the arrest and death of Jesus. In some towns, people drag chains around their feet or hold heavy crosses. Bands play sad music.

▼ A Good Friday procession in Minori, near Naples. People wear hoods so they cannot be recognized as they ask God to forgive their sins.

◄ In Naples people make a special Easter pie called *La Pastiera*. It is filled with sweetened *ricotta* cheese, candied citrus, and a little orange essence.

CASSATA ICE CREAM

Cassata ice cream was first brought to Italy by Arab cooks. Nuns copied the recipe and started making it as a special Easter treat. But in the seventeenth century they were banned by the bishop from making *cassata*. He thought they were spending too much time in the kitchen during Holy Week.

The nuns passed on the recipe to their friends, and soon *cassata* was being enjoyed all over southern Italy.

Easter Sunday

Easter Sunday brings a change in mood. Church bells ring loudly to celebrate Christ's rising from the dead. The time of fasting is over.

Many Italians have a special family dinner. In Naples, there is usually an *antipasto* of cold meats and pickled vegetables. It is followed by a special Easter *brodo* or soup, with noodles. The main course is roast lamb, served with side dishes such as fried artichokes and potatoes.

Easter cakes, cookies, and candy

In northern Italy, the traditional Easter cake is shaped like a dove. It is called *colomba di Pasqua*. Some people make chocolate cherry cookies. Others buy *schiacciata di Pasqua*, a cake made with eggs and butter. Children have chocolate Easter eggs too. The best ones come from the city of Perugia, and most have a surprise toy or chocolate inside them.

▲ This Easter lamb is made from almond paste. The lamb is one of the Christian symbols for Jesus.

◄ *Cassata* ice cream gets its name from the Arabic word *quas'at*. It means "large, round bowl." Find out how to make it on page 29.

Cassata Siciliana

INGREDIENTS (serves 6)

- 1 large container of vanilla ice cream
- Red and green food coloring
- 2 oz. (55 g) Glacé cherries, chopped
- 2 oz. (55 g) candied fruit, chopped
- 2 oz. (55 g) pistachio nuts

EQUIPMENT

Mixing bowl	Fork
Wooden spoon	Chopping board
Loaf pan	Knife
Plastic wrap	

Allow one third of the ice cream to soften a little. Put in a drop of red food coloring and beat until the ice cream turns red. Mix in the fruit.

Line the loaf pan with plastic wrap. Pour in the softened ice cream and pat into a neat layer with a wooden spoon. Return to the freezer until it hardens.

Soften the next third to make a white layer, returning it to the freezer in the same way. Soften the last third. Add a drop of green food coloring and mix in. Stir in the nuts and pour into the loaf pan.

Return the mixture to the freezer. When it has set, turn it out onto the chopping board. Pull off the plastic wrap and cut the ice cream so that everyone gets a slice with three colors.

Always be careful with knives. Ask an adult to help you.

Glossary

Antipasto A starter course, served before the main meal.

Cured Preserved by salting or smoking.

Fast To go without certain foods, or not eat at all.

Fertile Land that is good for growing crops is fertile.

Fertility Being fertile.

Gospels The first four books of the New Testament of the Bible—Matthew, Mark, Luke, and John.

Holy Week The week before Easter Sunday.

Honor To show great respect for.

Liqueur A flavored, sweetened alcoholic drink, to be drunk after a meal.

Mass A Roman Catholic service with a ceremony that celebrates Christ's death and his coming to life again.

Nativity The birth of Jesus Christ.

Patron saints Saints who are seen as the special protectors of a country, church, trade, or person.

Saints People whose holy deeds in life are recognized by a Church, especially the Roman Catholic Church, after they die. People honor them on special saints' days.

Photograph and artwork acknowledgments
The publishers would like to thank the following for allowing their pictures to be used in this book:
Anthony Blake Photo Library 14, 16 (above), (Tim Imrie) 27, (John Sims) 28 (above); Britstock (Eric Bach) 9, (Tschanz) 11; Cephas (Franck Auberson) 22 (left); Getty Images (Chris Windsor) *cover photo*, (Andy Sacks) 6; Chapel Studios (Alistair Beckett) 7 and 10, (Zul Mukhida) 16 (below), 20, 24 and 28 (below); Food Features 19; Robert Harding (John G. Ross) 18 (right), (Mike Newton) 26; Hutchison (Nancy Durrell-McKenna) 5 (bottom left), (Robert Aberman) 8 (both), (Gail Goodger) 18 (left); Norma Joseph 13, 22 (right); Kronos 2000 15; Pictor International 12, 23; Wayland Picture Library 5 (top right).

While every effort has been made to trace copyright holders, in one case this has not proved possible.

Fruit and vegetable artwork is by Tina Barber. The map artwork on page 4 is by Peter Bull and Hardlines. The step-by-step recipe artwork is by Judy Stevens.

Books to Read

Allen, Derek. *Italy* (Country Fact Files). Austin, TX: Raintree Steck-Vaughn, 1996.

Berg, Elizabeth. *Italy* (Festivals of the World). Milwaukee, WI: Gareth Stevens, 1997.

Boast, Claire. *Italy* (Next Stop). New York: Heinemann Library, 1998.

Borlenghi, Patricia. *Italy* (Country Topics for Crafts Books). Danbury, CT: Franklin Watts, 1994.

Harvey, Miles. *Look What Came from Italy* (Look What Came From). Danbury, CT: Franklin Watts, 1998.

Haskins, James. *Count Your Way Through Italy*. New York: First Avenue Editions, 1992.

Powell, Jillian. *Pasta* (Everyone Eats). Austin, TX: Raintree Steck-Vaughn, 1997.

Index

Page numbers in **bold** mean there is a photograph on the page.